Tales from the Past

By Peter Sawyer

Accompanying book for
Peter Sawyer Living History

To the pupils & staff of Beech Hill Primary

Yours historically

Peter

alias Areodotos

Αρεοδοτος

With thanks to all the pupils who have met Areodotos, Pamphilos, Valerius, Swithin, Tørvald and Peter

And all the teachers, headteachers, staff and others who have supported Peter Sawyer Living History

First published by Amazon 2020
First Edition

ISBN 9798676271312
Independently published via Amazon

www.peter-sawyer.com

Contents

There is a Help Section guide to the names, historical facts and foreign words after each set of stories.

Ancient Sparta
Areodotos of Sparta

Last day of summer, 420BC, Sparta, Greece

The last of the sacrifices and prayers had finished and the herd of fifteen boys had been checked once more that they wore nothing except short chitons tied with rope and carried only a short knife.

As soon as the signal was given, Areodotos turned left and began to run. The last stage of agoge was brutal and competitive and a good base before sunset might be the difference between success and freezing. The evening was already cold and, with not a cloud, only going to get colder still.

For some days, several other boys had talked about where they would go and what they would do. Areodotos had listened and soaked in everything that was said. His ability to remember was a gift of the gods, his tutor had said. Areodotos had learned to use it well. Almost all of the others were planning to go west beyond Pitana or towards Gytheio.

Areodotos went east to the river Eurotas and turned north, the city away to the left, Mount Taygetos towering over the houses, the temples, even the acropolis at the heart of the city. A helot house nearby had a dog and it began barking. Areodotos thought about killing it but chose to remember the fact and carried on along the river.

In the little free time he had during the summer, he had been scouting places to go and places to stay. Further up the river, it bent around like a horseshoe. Opposite was a sharp rise in the ground. On the north side of the little hill was a cliff, a bit higher than a man, overhanging to make something like a shallow cave. It was two stade from the nearest house and out of view of anyone following the river or the Corinth road, protected from the wind that came up the Spartan valley from the sea or off of the hills.

From the olive trees that ran up the hillside, he gathered enough wood to start a small fire with his knife and a stone providing the spark. First tasks in the morning, he decided, a cloak, some meat, perhaps some sandals. He looked up at the sky. The sun was well down, the sky itself a dark purple, the first stars beginning to appear, a sliver of moon just visible. A long time before, a young boy still at home, his mother had said that the moon changed as Phoebe chased her brother Phoebus across the sky each night. Having been in the agoge for almost twelve years, Areodotos had only faint memories of his mother, a woman with very pale hair for a Spartan but with dark eyes and a calm smile. His father was even more of a distant memory; as a captain of Sparta, Pylenor had often been away from the city fighting Persia or Athens. When he came home, he had been an impressive figure in his golden armour, scarlet cloak and with his spear in his hand and it had the effect that every Spartan father wanted: making his son want nothing more than to follow his father through the agoge and into being a warrior of Sparta. In the herd, Areodotos had been noted for his mind and his memory: he was not the tallest, strongest, fastest or loudest boy but he was smart, and he was able to watch or listen to something and then copy it. He could listen to the tales of Hercules and Achilles and repeat it almost to the word. It only took one demonstration of a skill for him to do it himself. A set of directions given to the boy would produce him at the place and time. It was part of his decision to be as good a Spartan as his father: that he devoted everything he had to whatever he was doing.

The night was colder than he thought it would be. Areodotos sat as close to the fire as he could, feeding it with fresh wood only when he needed to, so he did not need to keep going for more fuel. He shivered, began counting stars and waiting for sunrise.

'I doubt they are right.'

The sound of a voice startled Areodotos awake. He had dozed off, head against the rock behind him, the fire had all but burned out.

'The problem is that a citizen tells you that the sky is gold. If you say he is right, he beats you for lying. If you say he is wrong, he beats you for arguing.'

Helots.

Areodotos took his knife from the ground in front of him, where he had stuck it the previous night. Part of the agoge was to kill helots without being caught. Two might be a little ambitious for a first attempt but he decided to see.

There were two of them, men a little older than him, one with a severe limp and walking with a stick. They veered off of the road towards the river. Areodotos made sure that nobody else was in sight and slipped across the road, following his two targets. They were talking about something to do with a fishing boat that they had argued with a Spartan citizen about. The man with the limp stopped and sighed.

'Forgot the bait.'

'I can go back,' said his friend. 'You stay here, keep walking on that injured ankle and you will end up stuck in the house.'

'Are you sure, Agreus?'

'Sure. Back soon.' The man called Agreus turned back, leaving the limping man alone. He sat down on an olive tree stump to wait.

When Agreus returned, Laios was on the ground, bleeding from the neck.

'Laios! What in Zeus's name happened?'

Laios was hardly able to raise his hand before the young Spartan appeared from the trees and cut open Agreus's throat.

Back at his campsite, Areodotos checked his new items: Laios's sandals were a good fit but he kept the other pair too; the two cloaks, one hooded and one not, were thin linen but better than none; the walking stick was four feet long and solid; Agreus's knife was a little longer than his own although not as sharp. He had also recovered the bait, some hard and rather stale cheese but it was welcome.

Areodotos sat down and began to sharpen the knife with a stone while eating the cheese and an overripe fig that Laios had been carrying. He then took some time to sharpen the end of the walking stick and harden it in the fire. A trip to the river for a drink before he settled down to wait for nightfall.

The house with the dog was a normal Lacedaemonian farmhouse: built around a courtyard with enclosures for the animals surrounded by wooden fences or stone walls. The dog was around the back and, from the sound of it, it was a big animal. There was at least one girl about eight years old, feeding the ducks that were kept near the front door and carding wool, and a woman, who came out a few times as if looking for something. Areodotos wondered if he had killed her husband that morning and she was waiting for him.

The dog came trotting around the house. It was huge, with the mien and greyish brown fur of a wolf, and Areodotos muttered some appeals to Artemis under his breath.

He began forming a plan. He needed food, as much as he could, so it must be light and easy to carry: hard cheese, figs, perhaps bread if there was any. The girl would be no difficulty, the woman perhaps, but it was the dog that worried him. It was dark enough and he made his first approach. Three ducks died with barely a flutter or squawk and he cut them open quickly before retreating behind the wall. It was only a few moments before the dog came loping around the house, scenting the blood, its nose in the air. It leaped the wall and the ducks scattered. The dead ducks drew it across, it sniffed a few times and, despite a farm hound being trained to ignore live animals, gave into its nature and began to eat. The bones crunched in its mouth as it dug its teeth in.

As slowly as he could, Areodotos slid up and over the wall with the longer knife in his hand. The dog's back end was just a few cubits away. He was a third of the way there... half... two thirds...

'Koutavi!' The woman called from the door. 'Koutavi! Stupid dog, where are you? Kati, go and find the dog.'

The girl came out past her mother, looked around and went the wrong way, calling: 'Koutavi! Koutavi! Come here!'

With them distracted, Areodotos had creeped around to the back of the house. A water barrel was well-placed for him to climb up onto the almost flat roof. He could see the pantry opposite; he was on the wrong side of the house. The girl was still calling so he barked loudly.

'He's around the back!' her mother told her and, as the two went around, Areodotos crawled like a spider across the roof at the front of the house, around to the pantry side and dropped into the courtyard. Two pieces of bread, three figs, a piece of hard goat's cheese the size of his hand and another slightly bigger went into one of the cloaks, which he tied in a bundle.

'He isn't here!' the girl protested.

'I heard him bark. Keep looking around here, I am going to fetch a lamp.'

Areodotos tied his parcel to his back with the other cloak, jumped up and scrambled onto the roof, just as the woman entered the courtyard. She looked tired and worried in the light from the burning torch by the door. She went across to another room and returned with a lit oil lamp. As she did, she looked up towards the roof. Areodotos stayed absolutely still, confident that the darkness hid him. She did not stop and went back out of the door, calling for the dog again.

To stay away from her, Areodotos spider-crawled towards the back of the house, climbed up onto the higher roof and along. The girl's footsteps and voice were awfully close. She was talking to herself, calling the dog stupid, her father late and her mother bossy. Suddenly she stopped talking and Areodotos was sure that he must have made a noise. He froze again.

'Kati! I've found him!'

'Thank Hestia!' She hurried to find her mother.

As soon as she was gone, Areodotos dropped to the ground and started back towards his campsite, ignoring the noise of mother and daughter crying over their slain dog.

*　　　　*　　　　*

'Areodotos.'
Eumenes, the biggest boy in the herd, inches taller than Areodotos, broad across his shoulders, dark hair curling around his ears. He had been building up the fire.
'Were those two helots by the river killed by you?' When he got no response, he shrugged. 'Looked well done, came this way, saw the fire, thought it was you or Deinias.' Again, no reply.
'Now, you need to find a new campsite. This is mine.'
Areodotos had retrieved his sharpened stick and he aimed the point at Eumenes.
'I'm not scared of a stick. Especially not one that you're holding.'
Areodotos took a few steps forwards, swung his stick around in his fingers and held it out pointing to his side, a stance he knew Eumenes favoured.
The larger lad pulled his knife from the back of his belt. 'I'll gut you if I have to. I don't want to.'
Areodotos took a few steps closer to the little rocky outcrop that sheltered the campsite, not taking his eyes from Eumenes.
'This is stupid. Just walk away.'
Areodotos took another step. Eumenes sighed and advanced a step, switching the knife to point downwards. He raised it.
Areodotos quickly swung his wooden spear down, got the blunt end into the fire and flicked the burning wood at Eumenes. The larger lad stepped back rapidly and looked to attack but

Areodotos jumped onto the rock and leaped off, leading with the sharp end of the spear.

Eumenes dodged the point but got caught by Areodotos's elbow. He fell backwards, banging his head on the ground. Areotodos stamped on his wrist, ripped the knife away and threw it a short distance away. Eumenes tried to grab his ankle but he hopped aside and kicked his fallen enemy in the side. Again, Eumenes reached for his ankle but missed and got kicked in the top of the head. And then he was scrambling to get to his feet and tried to run away but Areodotos's spear spiked into the back of his knee. Just as quickly it was pulled out and spiked into the other. Eumenes went down in a heap.

Areodotos came around in front of him.

'Foolish little boy. You are little in your mind, even though you are big in your body. You think that anyone smaller or lower than you, without the thick muscle in their shoulders, is less than you. I am Areodotos, the gift of Ares. And Ares gives you more than strength and power. He gives wisdom, he gives reason, he gives skill and he gives planning. I knew I could use the fire before you spoke. I knew I could use the height to come down at you before that. I knew that I am faster than you and that you will always try to make the small ones smaller by tripping. I could kill you, Eumenes. I would be right to. You turned on one of your own, not on one of the others, and that gives me the right to kill you. But while you were skulking here, waiting to take my camp from me, I was out doing as we are supposed to be doing.'

The voices of the helot search party were growing louder. Eumenes heard them for the first time and looked terrified. 'You can't.'

'I can. I am going to let them find you. They'll blame you for killing their friends by the river and the dog at the farmhouse. They'll beat you, tie you like a goat and drag your back to the elders. And the elders will beat you harder and exile you from Sparta. If you are lucky, you might reach Corinth or Thebes. Or you might get eaten by wolves, only the gods can say.'
He found Eumenes's knife, which he added to his own, made sure there was nothing left and turned to leave after one more sentence, the most powerful insult: 'You are no Spartan.'

The Labours of Heracles

Heracles was one of many sons of Zeus but his mother wasn't Zeus's wife Hera, she's a human princess. After being driven mad by Hera, his very jealous and very angry stepmother, Heracles killed his wife and children. When he recovered from his madness, he went to the Oracle of Delphi to find out how to make things right. The priestess sent him to serve Eurystheus, King of Tiryns. He sent Heracles to perform ten tasks:

First- kill the Nemean Lion. The Nemean Lion was cursed by the gods. It was once a woman but now, whenever a man approaches, it turns into a lion and eats them. Hercules sharpened his sword and went into battle. He attacked the lion outside its cave, but its hide could not be pierced. Heracles forced the lion back into its cave, blocked the main entrance and sneaked in through a small hole. He stunned the beast with his club and using his great strength, he strangled the lion. He tried to skin it, but the hide was too tough. Eventually, the goddess Athena, his aunt and the goddess of hunting, showed him how to use one of the lion's claws to cut through the skin. When Heracles returned to Tiryns, wearing the impenetrable lionskin as armour, King Eurystheus was terrified, commanding Heracles to never enter the city again, only to display his trophies outside. He even had a giant bronze pot made, so he could hide from Heracles. He warned the hero that the labours will get more and more difficult.

Second- the Lernaean Hydra. This animal had been raised by Hera to kill her stepson: a poisonous monster with many heads. Wearing a cloth over his mouth to protect against the fumes, Heracles tried to kill the monster but every time he cut off a head, a new one grew. One night, after trying and failing, Heracles went to his nephew's house. His nephew, a very clever man called Iolaus suggests burning the necks shut. So, next day, as Heracles cut off a head, Iolaus burned the neck so that the head cannot regrow. When all the heads were cut off, the monster died.

Third- the Ceryneian Hind. This white deer was Artemis's sacred animal and Eurystheus knew that it was faster than an arrow. He forbade Heracles from killing it, saying it must be returned alive. Heracles chased it for an entire year all across Greece until he managed to trap it with a net. As he carried the hind back, he was confronted by Artemis, who forgave him for capturing her deer. After showing it to the King, Heracles released it back to its mistress.

Fourth- the Erymanthian Boar. Larger than a horse, this great boar was said to be unstoppable. Heracles chased it through thick snow until the animal became exhausted and then he was able to catch it. Eurystheus was so terrified of it, that he hit in his bronze jar until Heracles released the animal.

Fifth- Augean Stables. Cleaning the great stables of King Augeas was supposed to humiliate Heracles as the cows in the stable were enchanted and there were over a thousand, so their dung formed huge piles, filling the massive stables. Heracles knew that he couldn't shovel the dung fast enough, so he diverted the river to wash the stables clean but Eurystheus claimed this was cheating and that there were still seven labours to do.

Sixth- Stymphalian birds. These birds had bronze beaks and sharp feathers as well as poisonous dung and breath. They ate anything, including people. Heracles used a great metal rattle to scare the birds into the air and killed them one by one as they landed. Most then flew away but Heracles kept two to prove his success.

Seventh- The Cretan Bull. A giant bull large enough to knock down houses was terrorising the people of Crete. Heracles surprised the sleeping bull, choked it until it was senseless, tied it up and took it back to Tiryns. Eurystheus wanted to sacrifice it to Hera but she refused to accept something that Heracles had caught, so he released it into Marathon. The Bull of Marathon is attached to another series of Greek legends, the story of Theseus.

Eighth- Mares of Diomedes. The four man-eating horses of King Diomedes were mad and savage, but Heracles chased them onto a spit of land, quickly digging a trench to make an island. He then killed the evil king Diomedes and fed him to his own horses. This calmed the horses; Heracles tied their mouths shut and led them back to Tiryns. Once their master was gone, they became permanently calm and Heracles kept one, Deinos, as his own horse.

Ninth- Belt of Hippolyta. King Eurystheus wanted the belt of the Queen of the Amazons as a gift for his daughter, Admete.

Hippolyta had heard of the great hero and was willing to give him her belt if he stayed and told his story, but while he did, Hera disguised herself as an Amazon and started a rumour that Heracles was going to kidnap Hippolyta. The Amazons attacked Heracles, who accidentally killed Hippolyta in the battle and fled with her belt.

Tenth- Geryon's Cattle. Geryon was a monster with three heads, six arms and three legs but Heracles was too strong and killed him. Hera sent flies to drive the cattle mad and it took Heracles a year to round them all up. She then flooded a river to stop him getting back to Tiryns, but Heracles piled stones in the water until it was shallow enough to cross.

Eleventh- The Golden Apples of the Hesperides. After doing ten labours, Eurystheus insisted that the Hydra and the Stables did not count, as Heracles had help from his nephew and from the river. The Eleventh Labour was to steal the Golden Apples of the Hesperides. When he found the Garden of the Hesperides, he found Atlas, the Titan punished by Zeus to hold up the heavens. Atlas offered to get the apples from the Hesperides, his daughters, if Heracles held up the heavens. When he returned with the apples, he refused to take the heavens back. Heracles said Atlas could take the apples to Tiryns but first, Heracles must remove his sandals for comfort. Atlas put down the apples, took back the heavens but Heracles grabbed the apples and escaped.

Twelfth- Cerberus. The three-headed dog that guards the underworld was an impossible task, but Heracles was guided by Hermes, the messenger God into the underworld. Hades, Lord of the Dead, agreed that Cerberus could be taken if Heracles could subdue the animal without weapons. Heracles used his strength to knock the monster unconscious and carried it back. Eurystheus was so scared that he hid in his bronze jar and commanded Heracles to leave with Cerberus and never return. As soon as Heracles put down the three-headed giant dog, it disappeared back to the underworld.

Spartan help section

Acropolis- The centre of a Greek city, originally a fortress but normally a shrine to the gods.

Agoge- The Spartan national education, different for boys and girls. It started at 7 and ended at about 19. Boys had to leave home and go and live in 'herds' where they learned how to fight and survive. At 18, they had to leave the city and spend the winter out on their own, stealing and killing to survive. If they were caught, they had to leave Sparta

Agreus- Say Agree-us. Greek name meaning 'Hunter'. Very common in Sparta and Corinth.

Amazons- A mythical warrior people who were all women.

Areodotos- Greek name meaning 'Gift of Ares'. Say Ah-ree-a-dot-os.

Ares- The Greek God of War. Son of Zeus.

Athens- The largest city in ancient Greece. The first place in the world to elect their leaders.

Atlas- A Titan (immortal man) who rebelled against Zeus and the Gods. Punished to hold up the heavens on his shoulders.

Corinth- A Greek city which controlled a narrow stretch of land which connected the Peloponnese (where Sparta was) to Attica (where Athens is). Their city colour was pink.

Cubit- An ancient measure of distance, the distance from the tip of your elbow to the top of your middle finger. Roughly 40-45 centimetres.

Deinas- Greek boy's name meaning 'Terrible, Frightening'.

Delphi- The Temple of Apollo at Delphi had an Oracle priestess, where people, especially the Spartans, could go to ask the god's advice.

Eurotas- The river running past the town of Sparta.

Eurystheus- Say Your-is-they-us. A Greek boy's name meaning 'broad and strong'. Perhaps this is a bit of a joke, given what he's like.

Eumenes- Greek boy's name meaning 'Strong spirit'.

Gytheio- Sparta's port on the south coast, a helot village with the Spartan navy in the harbour.

Hades- Greek god of the Underworld, where you go when you're dead.

Helot- Helots lived in Sparta, but not actual Spartans. They did all the farming and making of things because Spartans were not allowed to.

Hera- Greek goddess of women, marriage and childbirth. The wife of Zeus and often takes revenge on her husband when he has other girlfriends.

Hermes- Greek god of messengers and travel. Escorted dead souls to the Underworld.

Hestia- Greek goddess of the hearth, home and family. Stepsister of Zeus.

Iolaus- Say Yo-louse.

Koutavi- Say 'Koo-ta-vee.' The Greek word for puppy.

Lacedaemonia- Spartans called their country 'Lacedaemon'. Say Lack-a-day-mon. Sparta was the city, Lacedaemon was the country.

Laios- Say Lie-oss. Greek name for a boy. Several kings in mythology were named Laios.

Persia- A huge empire that stretched from modern Turkey to Afghanistan and Iraq. Many Persian kings were keen to add Greece to the Persian Empire.

Phoebe- Another name for Artemis, goddess of the moon. Some Ancient Greeks believed that Artemis and Apollo chased each other through the heavens, which is why the sun and the moon rose and fell.

Phoebus- Another names for Apollo, god of the sun, he was the twin brother of Artemis. They often argued.

Pitana- One of the four villages that made up the town of Sparta.

Pylenor- Say Pie-len-or. A Greek name meaning gatekeeper.

Scarlet cloak- A bright red cloak was the mark of a Spartan soldier.

Sparta- Sparta was a small city in southern Greece. It was the first organised army in the ancient world, every Spartan man was a member of the army and were not allowed to be a farmer or craftsman. Girls were bought up to be strong and fit so they would have healthy babies. Spartans were known around Greece for being loud, aggressive, warlike and athletic.

Stade- One Greek stade is 192 metres. The first Olympic race was 1 stade.

Taygetos- A high, forest-covered mountain to the west of the town. Sacred to Ares and Artemis.

Thebes- Greek city close to Sparta. People from Thebes were thought of as boring and uncreative by other Greeks.

Theseus- Say Thee-see-us. An Athenian hero who killed the Minotaur.

Tiryns- A castle or citadel in southern Greece.

Zeus- Chief of the Greek Gods. Husband of Hera, father of Artemis, Ares and Apollo. God of thunder and lightning, leaders, justice and fatherhood.

Ancient Rome
Valerius Drusus Aprilis

2nd April AD 93- Litus Fretum (Saxon Strait/English Channel)

The fog was so thick that nothing could be seen beyond the far end of the boat. Thirty chained slaves were rowing in time to a beating drum while a Gaul soldier shouted insults at them. The two passengers, perched among the cargo at the front, were huddled under blankets and shivering.

'Why can't these Gaul peasants learn Latin?' one shouted to the other.

'He probably speaks better Latin than you do, Tiberius!'

'Oh, funny! Very funny from a man who doesn't even come from Rome!' Tiberius tried to stand up but the boat rocked and knocked him down again. 'I think I should have made a greater offering to Neptune! I cannot see anything but fog!'

The other passenger grabbed the side of the boat and pulled himself upright. 'No, only fog! How does the shipman know where to steer?'

'Neptune's hand and luck!'

'I do not wish to meet Neptune or Pluto today!' He turned around and staggered towards the mast at the centre of the boat. His blanket fell to the deck as he did, uncovering his jointed steel armour and the red tunic beneath it. He stumbled and the Gaul caught him.

'A problem, legionary?' he asked.

'How far to the coast, shipman?'

'Any time now. There will be lights on the harbourside to follow.'
'How do you know where we are?'
'I trust the gods, legionary. And tell your friend that I do speak better Latin than he does.'
The legionary laughed. 'He is not my friend, just another legionary sailing to his new post. But I will tell him.'

The shipman was right: soon a glowing fire showed through the fog and then a second. The shipman steered the boat straight to the centre and inside the stone breakwaters of the harbour.
'Dubrae,' Tiberius sighed. 'Britannia. It stinks like a dead pig.'
'It cannot stink more than the boat, get me off!' Figures loomed out of the darkness as ropes were thrown ashore. The legionary picked up his equipment- a cross shaped wooden frame with two leather bags strapped to it, sword and a cloth bag and stepped onto the harbour as soon as he could.
'Harbour prefect?'
'Who asks?' A man in legionary armour but with a small, round shield on his arm was standing nearby.
'Hail! I am Valerius Drusus Aprilis, newly assigned to the Second Legion.'
'I was told ten men were coming.'
'I was told ten. I found only three at Lutetia and they all took ill. Only I made it to the port and this far.'
The prefect sighed. 'You cannot walk to Isca Augusta alone.
Some Belgae with ideas of glorious rebellion would cut you apart and walk away in your armour.'
'I walked Aelia Capitolina in the dark and lived.'

'This is not Judea, this is Britannia. The house with the stone columns, by the temple, that is mine. Rest in the back room, I will see what I can do for you.'

There was a basin in the room, filled with fresh water and Valerius paused over it, catching his reflection: dark brown hair, equally dark eyes, a small nose, slightly downturned mouth and a chin badly in need of a shave. Arriving at his new legion looking like an escaped slave would be a bad first step but his razor had broken one morning in Gaul and he had been unable to find a new one. He splashed some water onto his face and sat down on the bed, resting his head on the wall behind. After travelling for ten days across Germania, then Belgica to the shore of the Saxon Strait and then across the sea to Dubrae, he was exhausted and considered falling asleep, but the prefect entered.

'Aprilis, I have a method of travel for you. A load of wine is heading to Londinium through Durovernum Cantiacorum. You could travel with it.'

'Is there a seat on the cart?'

'I am sure there is. Shield? Javelin?'

'I will collect them at Isca Augusta. I have a sword, a dagger, this is Britannia not Germania.'

'Safe enough.'

Valerius sighed and stood up. 'Where do I go?'

'I will show you.'

There were three horse-drawn carts loaded with huge amphorae of wine, three Celtic drivers and four legionaries, one holding a loaded pack donkey's rein.

'Hail. Valerius Drusus Aprilis, Second.' Legionaries commonly just used the number of their legion to identify where they were from.

'Spurius Titianus Albus, Ninth.'

'You're escorting the shipment?'

'We are.'

'I am heading to Isca Augusta, would you mind a travelling companion?'

'Not at all. My comrades: Cassius Aulus, Rufus Manius Vitus and Avitus Domitius Longinus is the thin one with the donkey.'

All four were carrying javelins and shields as well as swords and daggers. Their equipment was loaded on the donkey and Avitus took Valerius's things and added them to the load.

'Is it always so cold in Britannia?'

'First week of spring, you are lucky there is no snow.'

'I thought Moesia was bad.'

'Think how bad it was and add drizzling rain and Britons.'

Dubrae was little more than a village and the little convoy was soon in open countryside, still mostly hidden by fog. The air smelled damp and muddy, the road was uneven.

'Can the Ninth not build roads?' asked Valerius, tramping along at the rear with Spurius.

'We are based in Lindum not Londinium,' Spurius told him. 'There is only so far we can build. The roads west and north are better.'

'How is Lindum?'

'Fair enough. Better than it is further north. The Picts are unpleasant and the further north you go, the less pleasant they get.'

'I was told a little of Picts.'

'They appear like demons in the mist, kill as many as they can and run like rabbits. Pray to Mars that you do not see them. Although, it is better to see them and be ready than not see them and die. That happens far too often...'

'And they do not wear clothes!' Cassius, the youngest-looking legionary, called from his position on the right of the road. 'They fight with no clothes!'

Valerius snorted but Spurius nodded. 'It is true. I have heard far too many legionaries say so: the Picts fight with no clothes.'

'Brave or stupid?'

'There is a difference?'

They camped near Durovernum Cantiacorum overnight and then set out for Londinium, following the road across the marshes. It was mid-morning when they came across the rearguard of a group of legionaries.

'Hail! Who are you?' asked a man with a brown and black crest on his helmet, standing watch.

'Valerius Drusus Aprilis, *optio centuriae*, Second Legion.'

'Spurius Titianus Albanus, First Cohort, Ninth.'

'Marianus Seneca Proximo, *optio centuriae*, Third Century, Second Cohort, Ninth.'

'Bridge out?'

The man nodded. 'We have some men working on it.'

Spurius waved at the carts. 'Will they get across?'

'When we're finished they will.'

There were less than forty legionaries, three trees had been cut down and the soldiers were working on cutting planks with axes and daggers. Half a dozen were stood in the rib-high water checking the supports for the bridge, their armour and weapons on the bank. A few men stood watch while their comrades worked. The air was cold and there was rain drifting on the wind. The attack came from the far side of the river; over fifty Britons in bright tunics and trousers with large oval shields and long spears. The first group killed the unarmed legionaries in the river while the rest jumped or waded across. Roman weapons came to hand. With javelins laid aside, there was a drawn-out hiss as swords were unsheathed. Trained and experienced, the legionaries formed two walls of shields just as the Britons reached them. With no shield of his own, Valerius took a position behind the others.

The noise of the Britons colliding with the wall of Roman shields and swords was loud and unpleasant; a noise that even a veteran soldier like Valerius had never got used to: the combination of bodies hitting wood, steel cutting into bodies, war cries and shrieks of pain. The first row of Romans shoved forwards, their comrades pushing from behind. A Briton dived around the side of the Roman wall and almost ran straight onto Valerius's sword. Valerius kicked the dying man to the floor and turned to watch for danger but the Britons were running for the river again.

'To the bank!' ordered Marianus. The legionaries marched forwards, in two straight lines, trampling the dead and wounded enemies with their commander, Valerius and his companions behind. The last surviving Briton threw himself into the river.

'Hold! Check the fallen!'

The first row stayed in place, the second turned back to investigate the bodies left behind. One legionary had been injured, his neck gashed open; Avitus produced a bandage from a pouch on his belt and helped to apply it.

'All the men in the river are dead!' called one of the legionaries.
'This one is fine,' Avitus reported, tying the bandage. 'Try not to drink too fast, it may leak out, eh?' He tapped the wounded man on the helmet, grinning, and got a pained smile in return.
'They lost... fifteen,' said Valerius, counting carefully. The Britons were all wearing vivid red, bronze and blue tunics and several had check-patterned cloaks, most stained and bloody. 'If you want, I'll cross the river, stand watch on that side.'
'I will too,' young Cassius offered.
Marianus nodded. 'I doubt they will be back, but that may be best. Pius! Antonius! Get in that river and check those supports. Everyone else, back to work!'

They were across the bridge by mid-morning and continued north-west towards Londinium. The sun had finally burned away the last of the mist but Valerius was still glad of the short trousers beneath his tunic.
'Where are you from, Valerius?' asked Rufus.
'Child of the Legion. My father was from Parusia, fought in the Eight, then the Tenth, rose eventually to be a Camp Prefect. He retired to a farm near Parusia and when I wanted to join the army, I was sent to the Tenth.'
'Judea?'
'Judea. Aelia Capitolina.'
'Said to be one of the most dangerous cities in the most dangerous province in the Empire,' said Spurius.
'Not far away. The Judeans are Roman citizens, the same as you or I, but refuse to accept it. They spit on your shadows as you pass, steal your coin and deny it to your face, the man serving bread in the eating house stabs your comrade in an alley the next

day. And all protected by their cursed priests. They study our laws like there is nothing else. You use wooden swords to beat back a crowd, they protest citing the Augustan Laws. You surround a merchant's property for evading taxes, they protest. Then there are the Zealot rebels, ambushing patrols with slings and daggers, slaughtering horses in the night, poisoning wells. And if you attack on their holy day, their damned priests protest to the governor.'

'Sound pleasant,' Rufus observed.

'Oh, Judea is. I forgot the dust, the heat and the *awful* food. You have truly not lived until you eat fried camel for a week. Finally, nearly a whole cohort was moved to Rome for a few short weeks before being sent to the Fifth Macedonia in Dacia and Greater Germania.'

'And so, it gets better,' Spurius observed sarcastically.

'Oh, indeed. Rain. More rain. Then after the rain, it rains again. The Dacians are like the Britons, emerging from the mist, but they come thundering in with great two-handed scythes that can cleave through a helmet. The Judeans sneak and spy and lie; the Dacians are as sneaky as a bull wearing armour. They scream and shout and it is like being attacked by a herd of bears.'

'Which did you prefer?' asked Cassius, taking the mule's rein to allow Spurius a rest.

'The Dacians! Judeans are slimy, ratty little things, at least Dacians stand and fight and they are honourable in their own mad, ale-soaked way.'

'Why send you from Germania Superior to Britannia?'

'It was supposed to be ten of us, *optio centuriae* and *signifiers.* But only three were waiting in Lutetia and they all took ill before we left, so I have travelled from Lutetia alone...'

28

'One man in place of ten, you will have to fight like Mars himself.'

'And carry three or four standards as I do. I can barely carry one without fighting at the same time!'

'Family?'

'My parents are gone. My sister, Julia, is the wife of a well-meaning but somewhat stupid olive oil maker.'

'I have a brother who makes oil,' said Cassius. 'In Malaca in Hispania. And a sister who is a mother of five children.'

'Malaca too?'

'Nearby, yes.'

'You are Hispanic?'

'I am. Proudly so.'

Valerius snorted. 'I'd be prouder of being a duck or a fig tree.'

The other three laughed. 'Spurius? Where are you from?'

'Brundisium, south of Rome, eastern coast.'

'I have been. Something of an amphitheatre there, I was there for a Saturnalia festival. Rufus?'

'Child of the Legion: Twenty-Second Primigenia is in my father's soul and my mine. A man of Rome, discharged in Mogontiacum, married a local girl. I grew up in the village beside the fort and joined as soon as I could but I was in the Twenty-Second Pri for only a year before being sent here. That was four years ago.'

'Avitus?'

'Avitus is a barbarian,' sniggered Cassius.

'Says a man from Hispania,' Avitus retorted. 'I was born in Lindum. I was raised an orphan by a Pict. I took the Military Oath as soon as I could, I wanted to be more than a Roman orphan in Lindum. I was an auxiliary, an archer, and they

29

drafted hundreds of us into the legion. Now, I want to be a centurion, even a Camp Prefect.'

Valerius suddenly noticed how much older Avitus was than the others, perhaps almost forty despite his thinness.

'You are a barbarian, Avitus. You have more chance of being a Vestal Virgin,' said Spurius. 'No tribune would make you a centurion. And who would recommend you? Even if you served until you were eighty, there would still be nobody who would make you a centurion.'

'I will prove you wrong.'

'The day you become a centurion, I shall march into the sea,' Spurius promised.

9th April, Isca Augusta (Caerleon, Wales)

Almost asleep but still walking, Valerius Drusus Aprilis trudged through the Porta Praetoria of his new legion's fort behind the wheat cart, which he had followed for the last day. The gates were closed behind them. Every Roman camp was built identically, even if the materials varied: Isca Augusta had wooden buildings with tiles of grey slate, a wooden wall on top of an earth bank and the main avenue up to the headquarters was covered in chalk. The sounds of barracks, talking and shouted orders, clinking metal, axes on wood, were all familiar and comforting to Valerius. He raised a swifter walk up to the Principia headquarters building at the centre of the camp, the only one made of blocks of grey stones. Two legionaries, stood on guard at the door, stood to attention as Valerius approached.

'Camp Prefect?'

'Inside, second room.'

Valerius removed his helmet, ducked inside and found the second room. A distinctly elderly soldier, in just a red tunic and sandals but with a sword slung on his belt, looked up from his work.

'Soldier?'

'Sir. Valerius Drusus Aprilis, sent from Lutetia, transferred from the Fifth Legion Macedonia.' He handed over the documents he had been given to prove his identity and assignment.

'Ah, yes. How many with you?'

'I am all that made it to Britannia, sir.'

'One man.' The Camp Prefect, in command of the camp, a veteran soldier, frowned.

'Yes, sir.'

'Not a signifier?'

'No, sir. *Optio centuriae.*'

The Camp Prefect consulted a list. 'Second Century, Third Cohort. Centurion Pontus Flavius Gallus. Right back near the gate.'

'Sir.'

Valerius somehow kept moving all the way to the gate. The barrack blocks were long, log-built and slate-roofed each one with five doors facing the Via Praetoria.

'Centurion Pontus Flavius Gallus?' he asked a passing man and was pointed to the very closest door to the gate. *I need not have walked to the headquarters*, he thought to himself, *just introduced myself to the centurion and let him do the walking.* The doorway was covered by a curtain and Valerius knocked on the door frame.

'Yes?'

'Centurion?'

A gaunt man with, unusually, a shaved head pulled the curtain aside. 'Who are you?'

'Hail, Centurion. I am Valerius Drusus Aprilis, your new *optio centuriae.*'

'Oh.' The centurion, in just a working tunic and with a sandal in hand looked pleasantly surprised. 'Just you?'

'Is that a problem, Centurion?'

'I need twenty men, not just one. But one cup of wine is better than none.' He put his sandal on his foot. 'Come from the Ninth?'

'Fifth.'

'Fifth?!'

'I came from Mogontiacum via Lutetia. I was supposed to be with others but...' He shrugged and the centurion nodded. 'Who wants to come to Britannia? Amazing how many fall ill before their journey... could be worse though... No matter. We are a small century. Only fifty-two men, fifty-three now. Five are at Isca Dumnomiorum, two more in the hospital after seeing the same... anyway...' He led the way around the building, where there were five more doors. 'This is you. There are only three other men in your *contubernium*, all on guard duty at the stable. Javelin, shield?'

'I will need them.'

'I will send someone. You look tired. Rest, sleep, there is no pressure.'

'Thank you, Centurion.'

Taking off his armour for the first time in two days was an utter relief. There were eight wooden beds occupying almost all of the room. Valerius dropped his things beside one, spread out his blankets and was asleep within moments. He was shaken awake just before dark.

'Sir? Sir, I brought you some food.'

Valerius struggled to sit up. 'Who are you?'

'Publius, sir. Publius Marianus. I'm in your *contubernium*.' He handed over a pottery plate bearing cheese, a piece of bacon and crumbling bread.

'Thank you. Who are the other two?'

'Julius Arias Hadrianus and Quintus Desmus Alba, sir.'

'You're... Gaulish?'

'I am. This is my first posting, sir. I only finished training twenty days ago.'

'How do you like Britannia?'

'About as much as I liked marching through mud carrying weighted javelins, sir. And the camp prefect here likes to keep us doing that when we are not doing other things.'

Valerius laughed. 'I remember that too well. And you don't have to call me sir in here. Valerius is my name, use it. So, tell me of Isca Augusta.'

'It is much like any other camp.' Publius sat down, taking his helmet off and laying it on the floor. 'We do have an arena though.'

'An arena?'

'Right alongside, did you not see it?'

'I was so tired, I could barely see my feet.'

'An arena, the British village to the west side...'

'Dangerous?'

'Not in camp but the Britons have no respect for the Roman Peace so we patrol north in numbers. A month ago, the Sixth Century came north with us and set up a camp for a few nights. We went out to patrol the paths, we returned and the Sixth had been attacked by a large number. As we marched back here, we were attacked again. We lost twenty men, the Sixth lost almost fifty. The cursed Druids work their men up into frenzies and they fight like beasts. And to the north, the mountains hide them when they run.' The young Publius spat on the floor.

'My travelling companions from Dubrae said similar things of the Picts. I saw the like in Judea and Germania.'

'You fought in Judea?'

'Two years.'

'Bad?'

'What's the worst thing you can imagine? Imagine something worse. Then make the people doing those things Roman citizens. Then you get close to Judea.'

The curtain opened and two more young soldiers entered.

'Hail, *optio*,' they both said.

Valerius nodded. 'Valerius Drusus Aprilis.'

'Julius Arias Hadrianus,' said the taller, slightly shaggier one.

'Quintus Desmus Alba.' Smaller and built like a bull, very dark skinned and with very dark eyes. 'Welcome to Isca Augusta.'

By morning, Valerius had two javelins and a shield, a new pair of sandals and two new tunics, a brighter red than the Fifth Macedonia wore. At the morning parade, it was clear that the whole legion, not just the century, was short of men with perhaps only three and half a thousand men forming up instead of almost five thousand. Several men of the Second Century of the Third Cohort nodded to their new *optio* as he took his place in the centre of their last rank. The First Cohort, to the right, should have had ten centuries, eight hundred men, but looked to have barely five hundred. The Fifth Cohort, last but one on the left of the legion, had less than half of its strength. On the parade ground in the centre of the camp, the men of Legio IIA came to attention as the Camp Prefect mounted his podium.

'First, Third and First Cohort's Seventh Centuries, guard rotation!' he announced bluntly. 'Fourth and Fifth, fatigues. Sixth and First's Eighth, wall maintenance. All others, drill on the field and in the amphitheatre under the *tribunus laticlavas*.'

There was a stifled groan; tribunes were often rich, young and slightly useless, only serving time in the army before heading to a life of politics and luxury in Rome.

'Tenth Century, First Cohort: report to the stables. Second Century, Third and First Century of the Fourth, remain on parade. Centurions to me. Disciplinaries by noon. Centurions, conduct your roll, report to your tribune. Second Legion Augusta, *Roma victor!*'

'*ROMA VICTOR!*' roared the legion.

After the centurions had counted and registered their men, the parade was dismissed but for the Second Century of the Third Cohort and the First of the Fourth.

'Stand easy,' Pontus Flavius allowed his men to put down their shields, rest their javelins on them and flex their limbs as he went to the Camp Prefect.

'*Optio?*' A man in the rank in front turned about. 'I am Lucius Lironius, *tesserarius.*'

'Valerius Drusus Aprilis.' They clasped hands. The *tesserarius* was the *optio*'s immediate deputy, as the *optio* deputised for the centurion.

'Difficult journey?'

'Eventful. And lonely at times. Where is the signifier?' Every century had a standard bearer, who stood at the front of the century but there was nobody there for the Second Century of the Third Cohort.

'In the hospital, sir.'

'Should you not be in his place?'

Lucius Lironius shrugged and turned to the front as the centurion returned. '*Optio! Tesserarius!*'

Valerius and Lucius hoisted their shields and javelins and made their way to the front. 'Centurion.'

'There are reports of hostile Britons along the river to the east. We are to patrol up to the watchtower at Ceggapenn and reinforce the auxiliaries there for ten days until the First of the Fourth Cohort relieves us. Have the century prepared for ten days in the field: rations, tents, bedding and weapons. Ensure that we are prepared to leave by noon.'

'Aye, Centurion.'

'Yes, sir.'

'Go.'

The centurion turned back to the tribune. Lucius sighed. 'Ten days in the field. Mud and damp, *bucellatum* and sour wine.'

'Tents and bedding?'

'I can, *optio*.'

'I will see to weapons and rations,' Valerius nodded. 'How many *contubernia* do we have? Six?'

'Six.'

'I will have it done. Ready by noon.'

A few moments before noon, the Second Century of the Third Cohort formed up at the main gate. A man in chainmail armour over a green shirt and Celtic breeches was waiting, carrying a circular red and white shield but with a Roman gladius at his side. In marching column of five abreast, Valerius was alone behind the rear rank. He was pleased to see that Lucius Lironius had retrieved the century's standard and, although he was not wearing the *signifer*'s fur, he stood at the front. The centurion made no comment and exchanged some words with the Briton, who turned and strode out of the gate.

'March on!' ordered the centurion.

The roads had mostly been good legion constructions from Dubrae to Londinium to Isca Augusta. The road to Ceggapenn was a rough local track. The fifty-three men of the century marched on the grass to either side, Valerius in his position at the rear; Julius, Quintus and Publius were just feet ahead. Most of the soldiers had their helmets off, hanging on their chests from straps around their necks.

'Publius! What's the difference between a dead Briton and a live Briton?' asked Quintus.

The Gaulish recruit glanced back and sighed, expecting the joke. 'Tell me.'

Quintus dived forwards, jabbing the younger man just above his belt with the tip of his javelin. 'Living ones stick knives in your gut.'

'Jump in the river, Quintus!'

Quintus and Julius both laughed, so did some of the soldiers ahead. Teasing Publius was clearly a popular pastime. The junior soldier slowed to allow the others to pass him.

'I'd offer to sing,' said Valerius. 'But I only know Fifth Legion songs.'

'Not much call for those in Britannia, *optio*,' Quintus told him. 'And singing out here tends to attract the Britons.'

'It attracted the Marcomanni and the Quadi and the Cotini too, we did it anyway.'

'Sounds… stupid.'

'The Fifth did one thing and did that one thing very well. We weren't roadbuilders or garrison troops. We fought.'

'We fight too, *optio*.'

'I don't doubt it.'

'Still not recommended to bring the Britons down on us,' said another soldier, older than most of the others.

'Serginius is our resident expert on the natives of Britannia,' said Julius. 'Serginius is on his second tour.' This meant that Serginius had been in the legions for twenty-five years and, on discharge, turned around and re-joined.

'Yes, I'm the Olympian of Experts,' snarled Serginius. 'Yes, I'm more experienced than Mars and older than Saturn but I fought that murderer of children, the Iceni queen, Boudicca. I was at the 'Dacians too,' Valerius admitted. 'Personally, I thought it foolish but who am I to argue legion tradition?'

'How long were you with the Fifth?' asked Serginius.

'Almost five years. How far to Ceggapenn?'

'We should be there by noon.'

'Is it much to see?'

'A low watchtower guarding the mouth of the river,' Julius told him. 'Normally, there's a few maniples of auxiliaries there and a few sheep. But a tribe of Britons in that area, Silures who dislike the Roman Peace, who keep coming back at intervals to try and burn it down.'

'I can fight Quadi, what do I expect from Silures?'

'On ground like this?' Serginius waved at the gently flat grasslands that surrounded them. 'Chariots. They will try and break us apart, then the warriors jump off and attack with spears. The trick is to keep together, the horses pulling the chariots will not charge into a solid line of shields. When they tire of throwing things, they either run or they dismount. Then they are easy: get inside the spear, most barely have armour so they cannot protect themselves.'

Valerius nodded, trying to take in the details. 'Different.'

'Very, *optio*,' Publius assured him.

'What would you know, Publius?' Julius sneered.

'I can listen and compare two lots of information.'

'Publius is very proud of his great achievements, like listening to people,' Quintus chuckled and, suddenly, Publius lurched forwards bashed his javelin against the back of Quintus's head and then jumped on top of the other legionary, knocking him to the ground, still slapping him on the back of the head with his javelin. Half of the century waded into the fight to stop him. Quintus was yelling and trying to fight back but Publius seemed to have totally lost his temper and control. It took Valerius, Julius, Serginius and two others to pull him off. Valerius took away his javelin, sword and dagger as the centurion struggled through the men to the scene.

'*Optio,* what happened?'

'One of the men attacked another,' Valerius told him, indicating the still-restrained Publius and Quintus, who was sitting on the ground, bleeding from the back of his head and his nose.

'Name?' demanded the centurion.

'Publius Marianus, sir.'

'*Optio,* take him back to Isca Augusta. Financial penalty and duties levied, at your discretion. When you have him assigned, bring your escort back.'

'Sir.'

'Take Quintus back with you, get him to the medic.'

'Sir. Quintus, Serginius, you three,' Valerius picked out two of the more experienced-looking soldiers. 'With me.'

The extra equipment from Quintus and Publius was distributed through the century and the unhappy party of six turned back for the fort, Valerius stuck Publius's naked sword into his own belt.

'I'm sorry,' Publius announced after a short walk. 'I... you... you have done nothing but abuse me since I got here.'

'And you just shrugged,' replied Quintus, mopping at the blood on his head with the sleeve of his tunic. 'Should have said something!'

'How do you feel, Quintus?' Valerius asked.

'Like some idiot hit me with a javelin and then smashed my face on the ground a few times. I hope Aurelius can close this wound up.'

'It's not big, just bleeding a lot,' one of the other men told him.

'I'd say it is...'

'Like someone hit me with a javelin?'

'Fair.'

Valerius paused, listening.

'Sir?'

'Horse hooves?'

'On the road?'

'No.'

'Celts,' groaned Serginius. 'Speed up, gentlemen.'

The uncomfortable walk became a painful slow run, Quintus stumbling. Publius insisted on helping him along, taking his helmet and steadying him as he ran.

Serginius veered off of the road onto the higher ground alongside. 'Just one!' he called. 'One chariot, three men.'

'I can stop them,' said Publius.

'They'll ride you down!'

'No, they won't. I only have to take the horse down.' He seized a javelin. 'Run and I'll hold them.'

41

'Publius...' Valerius sighed. 'Not sure about this at all...'

'I can do it, *optio*. I... disgraced myself today. Let me earn my honour back.'

Something that no Roman soldier could refuse: the chance to regain his honour. 'Then may the Gods greet you as a friend, Publius.' Valerius returned his sword.

'Take my shield,' Quintus insisted.

'And give him all the javelins,' Valerius added. 'Publius... die well. Everyone else, down to the river, off of the road.'

Valerius shook Publius by the hand and then followed the others to safety.

Boudicca's Revolt

Boudicca was the Queen of the Celtic Iceni Tribe in 60AD, in the eastern part of the Roman province of Britannia. Her husband, Prasutagus, was the King and, when he died, the Romans insisted that Boudicca hand over her lands to Rome. When she refused, she was whipped and her daughters attacked.

Boudicca joined forces with the Trinovantes, who were the nearest Tribe. They decided to attack to the Roman city of Camulodunum, which had a large number of retired soldiers living there and a temple to the Emperor Claudius. Britons found this very insulting. The Roman legion normally based at Camulodunum was away across in Gaul, which is now France. Boudicca's Celtic army attacked the city and destroyed it, cutting off the head of the statue of the Emperor Nero. A part of the Ninth Legion from Lindum tried to take the city back but it was wiped out by the Celts.

The governor of Britannia, Suetonius, moved his army to Londinium (London). But Londinium had a no defences facing east towards Camulodonum, so Suetonius abandoned his positions and went north along Watling Street. The Celts burned Londinium down and killed everyone that they could and then marched north up Watling Street, destroying the next Roman town, Verulamium.

Suetonius managed to assemble an army of about ten thousand, made up of Legions Nine, Twenty and with some support soldiers. Boudicca's army might have been as large as two hundred thousand but was probably about half that size. Nobody knows where the battle was fought but was probably somewhere in Northamptonshire or Leicestershire. Boudicca probably gave a rallying speech, riding around her army in a chariot. The Roman Army fought in a very organised way, unlike the Celts. Suetonius reported over one hundred thousand Celts were killed and only 800 Romans.

Nobody is sure how Boudicca died. Some reports say that she took poison after the battle, she might have been killed in battle or she might have become ill and died soon after. It was the last time that there was a major revolt against the Roman Empire from within and the last time that there was an attack on Roman citizens by Celts.

Boudicca starts to appear in plays in Tudor England and then in poems. In Victorian times, she became connected to Queen Victoria, the poet Tennyson wrote an epic poem 'Boadicea' and several Royal Navy ships were named after her. In 1902, a very inaccurate statue of Boudicca and her daughters in a chariot was erected next to Westminster Bridge, across the road from the Houses of Parliament. Another was unveiled in Cardiff in 1916.

Roman help section

Aelia Capitolina- A city built by the Romans after they destroyed the Jewish city of Jerusalem in AD60. Now called Jerusalem.

Belgica- A Roman province north of Gaul. Roughly Belgium, named after its biggest tribe.

Boudicca- Say Boo-dic-ah. Queen of the Iceni, the Celts and lots of later Britons, she was a hero and a champion. To the Romans, she was a murderer.

Britannia- The large island now known as Britain.

Brundisium- A Roman port on the south coast of Italy, now called Brindisi.

Bucellatum- Hard biscuits that legions carried on the march. Extremely hard and not tasty.

Camp Prefect- The *praefectus castrorum* was in charge of running a Roman camp. Inside the walls, his word was literally the law.

Camulodonum- Roman capital city in Britain, now Colchester in Essex.

Centurion- The officer in charge of a century. Wore a red crest across his helmet. Centurions got important jobs for the Empire.

Century- A Roman army of 80 men, led by a centurion.

Cohort- A Roman army unit of about 480 men. Six cohorts make a legion.

Contubernium- A group of 8 soldiers who lived, slept, ate and fought together. We don't know if the centurion and optio were in the same one or different ones.

Dacians- Someone from Dacia, a land outside Roman control, north of Moesia.

Dubrae- A small Roman port, now Dover in Kent.

Duroverum Cantiacorum- A Roman village, now Canterbury in Kent

Gaul- A Roman province, roughly modern France.

Germania- A Roman province in what is now Germany. Divided into Germania Superior (the southern part) and Germania Inferior (the northern part). Most Romans hated Germania.

Hispania- The Roman province in what is now Spain and part of Portugal.

Iceni- A Celtic British tribe who were based in what is now Norfolk, Suffolk and Cambridgeshire. Known for fighting with chariots.

Isca Augusta- Roman legion fort. Now Caerleon in Wales. Isca Augusta had earth and wood walls and an amphitheatre next door. Named Fort Augustus, after the emperor Augustus

Judea- A Roman province. Now the southern part of Palestine.

Lindum- A Roman city, now Lincoln.

Londinium- The Roman city that is now London. Based roughly between The Strand and The Tower of London on the map.

Lutetia- Now the city of Paris in France.

Malaca- A Roman city, now Malaga in Spain.

Mars- The Roman God of War.

Moesia- A Roman province. Now parts of Serbia, Kosovo and Bulgaria. Some parts were very peaceful farming country but the eastern edge was very dangerous.

Mogontiacum- A Roman town next to a legion fort, now the city of Mainz in Germany.

Neptune- God of the Sea and Freshwater.

Ninth Legion- Legion 9 Hispania, based in what is now York and Lincoln. The 9th was the main enemy of Boudicca's revolt and had to be saved by the 20th and the 14th.

Optio Centuriae- The 'chosen man' of the century, second in command to the centurion. In charge of training and discipline.

Parusia- Now the city of Perugia in central Italy.

Picts- Picts were one tribe in Scotland but most Romans called anyone from northern Britain a Pict. It means 'painted' and is where we get the word 'picture' from.

Second Legion- Legion 2 Augusta, based in what is now Caerleon in Wales. Founded by the Emperor Augustus, has a Capricorn badge. 1 of 3 legions in Britain.

Signifier- A senior legionary who carried the legion's banner and in charge of the soldier's wages and pensions.

Silures- A British tribe based in south-east Wales. Some were very happy with Roman rule by this time but some still attacked Romans whenever they could.

Tesserarius - 3rd in charge of the century. In charge of the sentries and setting the password.

Tribunus laticlavus - Normally in charge of the legion, a young senator with big ambitions.

Twenty Second Legion Primigenia - One of the newest Roman legions, stationed in Germania Inferior. Known to be particularly good at fighting German tribes.

Pluto - God of the Underworld, where people go after they die.

Valerius Drusus Aprilis - Say Val-air-ee-us Droo-sus Ap-ril-iss.

Verulanium - Important Roman city in Britain, now St Albans in Hertfordshire. It is still on the Roman road of Watling Street.

Via Praetoria - The main 'road' through a Roman camp from the main gate to the centre.

Viking
Tørvald Ragnarsson

AD811- Sæwinesbørg (West Coast of Norway)

'I'll hit you again.'

Tørvald raised his blunt iron sword back to a guard position. His hands, right arm, right shoulder and the left side of his ribs all hurt from his father's blows. Ragnar, bald on his head but with a black and grey beard that reached his chest, was holding a stave instead of a sword.

'No, you won't.'

'I will.' Ragnar jabbed the end of the stave at his fourteen-year-old son's head and swung at his ribs.

Tørvald parried the blow and stabbed at his father's ribs.

'Better.' Ragnar repeated the move but faster and again his son responded. 'Ah, better!' He tried again, faster, and added a second swing, which Tørvald fended off. 'Much better.' Faster, a second swing and then a hard kick, which caught his son totally unprepared. The boot hit Tørvald in the hip and knocked him down.

'That's unfair!'

'You think the Russ fights fair? You think the Franks or the Anglians fight fair?' barked Ragnar. 'You are a fool, boy!'

'But we're just training!'

'Yes, we are! Training is making you ready for war, Tørvald! That is its purpose! Get up!'

Tørvald, dark haired, long-limbed, scrambled to his feet and went on the attack, jabbing and slashing at his father, who was forced to defend himself and retreat a few steps. 'Good! Aggression, force! That is what wins battles but also...' He dodged aside and smacked his son across the back with his stave. 'Brains as well.'

Tørvald sighed and shoved his sword into his belt. 'Yes, father.'

'You are getting better, Tørvald... that is why I think you should come this time.'

'...Raiding?'

'Yes. The jarl wants me to lead his raids again this year and we will go south. I think you should come. You are old enough, strong enough, tall enough, the best way to train is to fight for real. That is what you want?'

'Yes, father!'

'Then get yourself home, the boats are being floated in the morning.'

Sæwinesbørg was on the north side of the fjord, protected from the landside by a series of steep cliffs and dense forests that enclosed a wide, shallow semicircle containing around seventy households, accessible only down a steep path from the west or from the water. Tørvald had been training with his father up in a glade in the forest and followed the path back. At the village gate, a single man stood on watch, a horn on his belt, a red and grey shield in his hand and a spear leaning against the fence.

'Tørvald Ragnarsson, where do you go?'

'Home, Gjurd.'

'Where's your father?'

'Stayed up in the clearing.'

Gjurd waved him past. The house of Ragnar was just the second from the gate, a longhouse with rounded corners, a door at each end, a thatched roof and an enclosure for the pigs and chickens behind it. Beside the door on the gate side hung Ragnar's black and blue halved shield and a slightly-smaller one with yellow and red quarters separated by black stripes.

'Hreithunn! Get me some food!' he shouted.

'Get it yourself, you lazy goat,' came the answering call from inside. Hreithunn, Tørvald's older sister by five years, came outside with a bucket and a basket. She was no taller than her brother, with lighter hair, a smaller face and greener eyes. A small bearded axe hung from her belt. She put the basket aside, tipped the bucket of water out and retrieved the basket. 'Come on, be useful, get the eggs.'

'Father wants me to go south with him.'

'With us.'

'I need to talk to Bjørn, I need a shield.'

'You will. And an axe bigger than that fishing hook you have under your bed.'

'I'm good with a spear.'

'Better an axe, a tool as well as a weapon.'

Tørvald shrugged and continued towards the centre of the village. A stream cut through the village and the smith's was built alongside. Bjørn, suited to his name of bear, was six and a half feet tall, covered in dark brown hair.

'Tørvald Ragnarsson! You come for your shield?'

'What... how did you know?'

'Because you are going with your father when he leaves, yes?'

'Yes, but how do you know?'

'Because all of Sæwinesbørg knows. You and Geir will go on your first trip when the ships leave.' Bjørn put aside the tongs that he was working on and went to the back of the forge, where several unpainted shields were stacked against the wall. 'Now, there is no boss on this one yet but try it.' He took the first and gave it to Tørvald. The shield had no boss or edge, just a handle across the central hole.

'A bit heavy.'

'Hm.' Bjørn took it back and handed over another.

'Better. It's about the size of Hreithunn's.'

'It is.'

Tørvald lifted it above his head and swung around into a protective position. 'I can use this. Silver cross, black and blue quarters.'

'You know.'

'I've always known, when I was barely old enough to stand, I knew.'

'You are a wise boy, Tørvald Ragnarsson. I shall have this ready before you leave.'

*   *   *

Through the next morning, the villagers drifted down to the beach on the eastern side of the village. Three longships had been pulled up above the highwater mark and work was beginning to refloat them, led by a particularly round and stubby man known as Ragnar the Fat.

'Ragnar the Eagle, get those children of yours and help right the last ship!'

Tørvald's father nodded and waved him and Hreithunn towards the smallest of the three ships, the only one still on its side. Ropes were being attached to haul it upright and pull down into the water.

'Tørvald, get up and get those ropes tied on the top of the mast,' his father told him. 'Hreithunn, the props.'

Tørvald scrambled up the mast to attach the ropes and clung on as the men pulled the ship upright, Hreithunn helped push the wedges in to hold the ship upright. With the vessel straight, Tørvald released the ropes and scrambled down. The crowd was growing as the ropes were retied around the stern posts and large round logs put in place between the ship and the shore.

In a wave of red-brown hair, beard and bear fur, Jarl Gudmund arrived with his family and guards. He was almost seventy years old and not as strong or as upright as he had been but was still somewhere close to Thor in Tørvald's eyes.

'Ready?' he boomed and Ragnar the Fat trundled over.

'Ready, my lord. Hands to the ropes!'

The strongest men and tallest boys took the ropes. Tørvald found a space by this father. Some of the old men pushed the first rolling log under the ship and several women kicked away the wedges as the first pull hauled the ship towards the sea.

Everyone not otherwise engaged pushed from behind. The ship was not heavy enough to need the effort but the symbolism of the village working together was important. As the ship passed over a roller, it was moved and within moments, the smallest of the ships reached the steepest part of the beach. The men ran aside as the ship slid down and into the water, cheered by the villagers.

'Ragnar the Eagle, Ivar, Gulbrand, pull the ship to the wharf,' ordered Gudmund. 'Everyone else, there are two more ships.'

The three men began to haul the longship along the shoreline by the ropes as everyone else went back to work on the largest vessel.

The boats needed seasoning before being used; they were left in the water until the timber expanded, gaps patched with new wood and fresh tar. When that was done, the masts had their jibs attached, the sails hung and furled and, finally, the figureheads repainted: a gold and red dragon, a gold and black wyrm and a blue and black eagle with silver eyes, which Tørvald had modelled his shield colours on. The entire village feasted together that night.

'Father?'

'Tørvald?'

'How do you know where to go?'

'Practice, lad.'

'Where do we go?'

'We sail south for two days and a night then west until we sight the coast. When we do, we turn south again. The coast there is rich with targets.'

'Have you ever lost your way?'

'Never.'

'How?'

'Because I was well-taught. And I will teach you.'

'You will?'

'Of course, I will. One day, my sword will be yours and you will stand where I do. You will need to know how to guide your men as I do mine.'

'Father...?'

'Get some sleep, Tørvald. Today is the day you become a man, you do not want to sleep through it.'

At daybreak, Tørvald was outside the house, practising with axe and shield against a fence post. Hreithunn came out of the house and watched, vaguely amused. She had her own axe already on her belt and a long spear with a thin head in her hand. Her shield was red and gold halved down the centre. Ragnar had left home early and was returning, sword on his left hip, axe on the right, something small wrapped in cloth in his hand.

'The tide is coming in, we will be leaving well before mid-morning,' he told his children. 'Get your things.'

Hreithunn spiked her spear into the ground, leaned her shield on it and turned back to the house.

'Tørvald, come here! I have something for you.'

He hung his axe on his belt. 'Yes, father?'

Ragnar handed the small package over. 'I had Bjørn make this for you. I wanted it larger but there was too much else to do.'

Tørvald unwrapped the linen. It was chain mail, about a foot long, a few fingers wide, backed with leather and with two straps holding the ends together. 'Oh! It goes...'

'Around the neck. I wanted it longer, covering your chest. Bjørn will have to finish it when we return.'

'Thank you, father!' Tørvald hugged his father.

Ragnar the Eagle, warrior of Sæwinesbørg, was not used to showing his emotions but smiled and put an arm around his son's shoulders. 'May it and Týr keep you safe, son of Dagrún. I do not want you joining your mother in Valhalla just yet. Get your things.'

The entire village gathered on the shore. At the wooden wharf, the three longships were moored beside each other, the smallest on the outside. Ragnar the Fat was one of the first aboard, clambering across to take mastery of the dragon-headed craft.

'Keep a good watch on my animals,' Ragnar the Eagle told the jarl's daughter. 'And do not forget that all of the hens will lay every day.'

The girl of eleven smiled and nodded. Gudmund patted his daughter's head and embraced Ragnar.

'Do yourselves and your jarl honour. Come home. If you do not, I shall watch for you when I reach Valhalla.'

'We shall return,' Ragnar told him. To the rest of the village, he announced: 'We shall all return!'

Tørvald had been standing and watching his father and felt a sharp blow to his shoulder. 'Hey!'

'Get your things on the longship, boy,' growled Gjurd. 'If you're not aboard before your father, we leave you behind.'

Tørvald seized his bag and shield and hurried to the ship. Hreithunn took his things and stowed them under a bench with hers. Then he noticed who they would be alongside: not as tall as him, a woman with absolutely black hair, sharp cheekbones and sky-blue eyes. The person in the town who terrified Tørvald more than the jarl or his father.

'Ivi.'

'Son of Ragnar.'

The little woman took her seat across the longship, the handles of her twin axes clattering against the seat. Ivi fought with no shield or spear, only her two axes, which she had named Lightning and Thunder. Ragnar's sword was named Heart-Strong. Hreithunn's axe was called Breaker.

Ragnar had drawn his sword and the people left on the shore- the old, the young, the weak, the sick and the craftsmen that the village could not do without- all cheered as he raised it. The dragon ship, then the wyrm, released their mooring ropes and moved out into the fjord. Ragnar cut the eagle-headed ship's ropes with his sword to symbolise their departure and leaped aboard as the current pulled the stern out.

'To your oars!' he called, taking the steering board at the stern from Hreithunn. She slipped onto the rowing bench beside Ivi. Tørvald seized the oar in front of him as Bjørn sat beside him. The ship, steered by Ragnar, followed the others towards the sea.

* * *

'Is that it?'

Hreithunn barely looked up. 'No.'

They had been sailing for six days, with good winds, fair weather and calm seas. With the blue and white sail billowing, Tørvald had climbed the figurehead to watch for the coast. He looked to the right; the wyrm-headed ship with its black sail was just in view. The third ship was further beyond it; the three had been able to stay together due to the good conditions. Most of the crew were sat on the benches or the edge of the ship. Thrónd had a fishing line out over the port side. Hlif was playing a bockhorn instrument made from a goat's horn sat beside the steering oar and Bui, her husband, was singing along, joined on the end lines of each verse by those who knew the song, including Hreithunn and Ragnar.

'There?'

Hreithunn peered around the figurehead. 'Land! Land!'

Their father, sat by the mask, got up and joined them. 'Land!'

Bjørn took up his horn and blew. A moment later, he blew again. The answering notes came back from the other boats and they began to steer closer together.

'Look for the rocks, the arch or the cross,' Ragnar told his children. 'We need to know where on the coast we are.'

'Yes, father.'

'Yes, father.'

Ragnar patted Tørvald on the shoulder, stroked his hand over Hreithunn's hair and clambered aft to take over the steering.

'Is that Northumbria?' asked Tørvald.

'No, that's further south. We need to know where we are before turning south again.' Hreithunn took her axe from her belt, borrowed a whetstone from Bjørn and began sharpening.

'You have been doing that all journey,' Tørvald noted.

'I have. And I will do it every time that I can until I need to use her or until I am asleep in my own bed.'

'Wise words, daughter of Dagrún,' said Bjørn approvingly. 'Listen to your sister, young man.'

'But she's a girl.'

'And that makes her no less than a man,' the big smith told him. 'If a man can fight, a woman can. If a man can swim, a woman can. If a man can speak sense, a woman can.'

'And a woman can bear children, no man can do that,' Hreithunn smirked.

'Men are stronger than women,' Tørvald objected. 'Bjørn or Bui could lift a cow, you couldn't.'

'And Ivi fights without a shield, I cannot do that,' said Bjørn with a shrug. He pointed. 'Look, the cross.'

On a rocky islet was a large wooden beam, as tall as a tree, with another tied across it a third of the way down. Tørvald shuddered looking at it; it made him feel uncomfortable.

'What's that?' he asked, pointing.

'The Christian symbol for their god,' said a man sat nearby. The longest, greyest of beards, the most watery of eyes and the most gnarled of hands in Sæwinesbørg belonged to Arnleif. He looked up at it and sighed. 'Like Thor's hammer or Odin's raven.'

'Which god?'

'The Christians only have one.'

'One?'

'One god.'

'How could one god be god of all things? How stupid!'

Arnleif shrugged. 'Ask a Christian. But never discount another's beliefs, son of Ragnar. The Christian will fight for his god as hard as you will fight for Thor. The Rûs follow different gods to us, the Saxons, the Franks, but that does not mean they do cling to their gods as we do to ours.'

'Thor is not a blanket to cling to,' Tørvald scoffed.

'Thor is a blanket to cling to as much as your blanket!' Arnleif corrected him sharply. 'Do not speak to your elders as you do, son of Ragnar, or I will use you as bait for the fish! Clear?'

'I am sorry, Arnleif Gunnarsson.'

The ship turned south, still with the wind. The other two ships were much closer, both within view.

'How much further, Arnleif?' Hreithunn asked.

'A day and a night perhaps.'

*   *   *

59

Tørvald woke to the sound of his father in conversation. He struggled out from under his blanket to find the sail lowered and the other ships alongside, several men holding each other's oars to stop the vessels from drifting apart. It was cold, cloudy and the wind was blowing towards the visible coast.

'I say we go ashore on the beach,' said Ragnar the Fat, waving straight ahead. 'Use The Dragon to take us there, anchor the other two.'

'But the river would take us a lot further inland,' argued Ivi, always a part of any talk of strategy.

'And makes a better position,' agreed Hrolf, brother of the jarl and captain of The Wyrm.

'Last time we were here... we came from the beach,' said Ragnar the Eagle, thinking as he spoke. 'The last year the jarl came, we did the same. River. A camp on the south side.'

Ivi whooped and made punching motions towards the coast.

'You had better take us in, Ragnar,' said Hrolf to the Eagle. 'Your ship draws the most water.'

'Can do. Shields out and to the oars! Push off, into the river!' Ragnar ordered. Every person aboard all three longships took their shields and hooked them onto the curved pegs on each side to form a higher, more defensive wall and protect the rowers as they then took oars. Arnleif went to the fore and banged several times on a drum until everyone was set to row.

'In!' he roared and the oars pushed into the water. 'Forwards!' He pounded the drum and the rowers pulled back together, propelling the longship forwards. Ragnar steered to the left and then back slightly as the rowers pulled together to the drumbeat. The noise of the sea became overcome by the creak of the wood of the oars and the grunting of the rowing Norsemen. Tørvald

60

was rowing right near the stern with his sister inside him, looking up at his father just an arm's length away.

'Where are we, father?'

'A small river in Northumbria. There are several small villages near here. An excellent site.'

'You know it?'

'I have been in this area... three... four times, yes, I know it.'

'We came here my first raid,' said Hreithunn.

'No, we were further south than this. That river leads to the town of Jorvik. This does not.'

'We attacked the church at Jorvik.'

'Yes, we did. It was like taking milk from an infant.'

By midday, Ragnar the Eagle was craning his neck, looking for a landing sight.

'Here,' he announced. 'Oars in!'

Arnleif stopped his drumming and the oars were raised. The longship was approaching a wide shingle beach on the outside of a bend in the river. A small stand of trees ran down to the water's edge on the far side and another on a low hill just inland.

'Here,' he repeated. 'Bjørn, see to the ship with me. Scouts out for a perimeter, everyone else will start on defences.

Tørvald gazed in wonder at the new land. The grass was a much paler green, the bank was a sandy-brown shingle instead of the grey-brown of Sæwinesbørg, the trees were not towering dark pines, a small brown bird took off across the longship's path as it drifted into the bank. There was a small bump as the ship hit the riverbed and Bjørn and Ragnar leaped ashore carrying mooring pegs and ropes. The others began to climb out, taking their shields and weapons. Tørvald dug into his things for the mail

that his father had gifted him and secured it around his neck
before taking his shield and vaulting overboard, splashing down
into knee-deep water. He hurried through the cold water lapping
the shore, crossed the narrow beach and up onto the long grass.
'Not too far, Tørvald,' warned Bjørn, using the back of his
axehead to hammer a mooring peg home, but Tørvald was
excited by the new land and kept on walking towards the low hill
just a hundred yards away, taking his axe from his belt as he
trotted on.

'Stay close, Tørvald,' warned Ivi, out on watch, axes in her
hands.

He kept walking faster, up the grassy slope, the top of the
grasses up above his knees, anticipating the view over
Northumbria. And then he could see it. The land swept away, flat
but wild, untouched, grassy and clear.

'Tørvald! Back here!' barked his father.

He took one more look and turned back. He never heard the man
come out of the long grass and the sword swing was straight at
his neck. It hit the mail there and the force of the blow helped
Tørvald turn the rest of the circle and hack into the Saxon's
unarmoured sword arm with his axe. The man screamed,
Tørvald stepped back and the next swing of his axe took the
clean-shaven man's head from his neck, sending it rolling down
the slope. The severed neck spurted blood like a geyser for a
moment and the body toppled.

Ivi, Hreithunn and his father reached him.

'Are you hurt?' asked Hreithunn.

'Are there more?' demanded Ivi.

'Why did you not listen to me?' growled Ragnar.

Tørvald checked his neck. 'Not hurt. I think he's a scout.'

Ivi continued on, looking for more trouble. Ragnar glared at his son for another moment and then his face softened. 'You killed your first man, even as he tried to kill you.' Tørvald, suddenly aware of the fact, nodded slowly. 'You left the camp despite being called back.' Ragnar suddenly reached down, put his hand against the severed neck to cover it in blood, and then wiped it hard across his son's face. 'Tørvald Iron-neck. Warrior of Sæwinesbørg.'

Viking help Section

Anglians- People living in East Anglia in eastern England. Originally from Germany but centuries before this story.

Bjørn- Say Bu-yurn.

Bockhorn- or Buckhorn. A musical instrument like a flute or a recorder made of goat horn.

Chainmail- Armour made of iron rings linked or riveted together.

Figurehead- The front end of a longship was carved into the shape of animals, monsters or just into a shape.

Franks- People living on the north coast of what is now France, Belgium and the Netherlands.

Geir- Say Gear.

Gjurd- Say G-yurd.

Heart-strong- Many Vikings named their weapons, treating them like a friend or a pet. Ragnar's sword is *Hraustligr*, which means heart-strong or determined.

Hreithunn- Say Hur-eye-thun-uh.

Jarl- The chief or lord of a village or a few villages. It might have been a title like King or Count or it might have been a status you could reach.

Longship- The fastest way of travelling in Viking times. Viking longships had high bows and sterns, a single sail and were very shallow so they could be taken up rivers. When the wind was too low to sail, the ships were rowed.

Northumbria- The northern part of England between the River Humber and Durham. A Saxon kingdom with its capital at York (Jorvik).

Odín- Chief of the Viking Gods and god of wisdom, stories, poetry, knowledge and death. He was accompanied by a raven, the symbol of wisdom, and a wolf, the symbol of death.

Ragnarsson- Means son of Ragnar. Vikings did not have surnames, so boys were called 'son of' their father and girls were called 'daughter of' their mother. Sometimes this was swapped around.

Rûs- People from Eastern Russia.

Saxons- People originally from southern Germany, who started living in Britain after the Romans left in AD450. By AD700, it's thought that more than half the people in Britain were at least partly Saxon.

Sæwinesbørg- Say Say-wines-bore-ge. Based on lots of small Viking settlements all along the coast of Norway.

The Eagle, the Fat, Iron-neck- Another way of telling Vikings apart was by a nickname. Sometimes these were good (like Ragnar the Eagle), sometimes how you looked (Erik the Tall) and sometimes they were just rude.

Thor- Viking god of storms and conflict. His symbol was his great hammer, Mjolnir.

Tørvald- Say Torr-vald.

Týr- The Viking god of war.

Valhalla- Odin's hall in the afterlife. Half of all warriors killed in battle went to Valhalla, a hall with shields for walls, an overturned longship as a roof held up by spears. An endless Viking party full of food, drink, stories and singing.

Wyrm- A Viking monster like a dragon without wings.

Peter Sayer

5th May 1361, Western France

'Why is it that the last few miles are uphill?'

'Nottingham is the same.'

'Oh?'

'You have never been?'

'Never.'

'You should. If only to pray at our cathedral.'

'The church of Saint Mary in Ware has always served me well enough.'

The two pilgrims, using their walking sticks to help them up the last part of the slope, pressed on. The town stretched out across the valley below.

'Welcome to Aix-la-Chapelle,' said Roger. The sandy-haired clothes-maker from Wollaton in Nottinghamshire took a deep breath. 'It's been a long walk.'

'And a short sail.' The boat between Dover and Calais was where Roger of Wollaton and Peter of Ware had met. Peter, taller than his companion, with dark hair and a bow and quiver of arrows as well as his huge backpack, studied the city from their high viewpoint. He had been planning to travel to Rouen but, on Roger's advice, had gladly agreed to the slightly longer journey to Aix-la-Chapelle together.

'Worth it.'

'Entirely.'

They continued onwards, down the steep slope towards the walled city.

'Strange to think I fought Frenchmen, now I'm walking into one of their cities.'

'Poitiers?'

'Crécy.'

'Ah, bowman, of course.'

'I suppose, with your hand, you can't shoot.'

Roger shook his head. An accident as a child had cost him three fingers on his right hand. 'It's why I chose to sew clothes instead of becoming a smith like my father.'

'Is that the cathedral?' Peter pointed to the huge structure rising in the centre of the town.

'It is.' Roger had been to Aix-la-Chapelle before. 'The dome in the centre is the nave. A man told me that it is modelled on the great basilicas of the Holy Land.'

'One day, I would like to go. But that is some voyage.'

'A shame there are no Crusades. A chance to fight the heathens and see the great sights.'

'I've done enough fighting. Is there a hostel in the town?'

'Right beside the cathedral. Does very fine ale and real mattresses.'

'What more could I ask for? Into the cathedral tomorrow, if they close the gates at sunset, we will barely be inside.'

'Fair enough.'

The gatehouse was of brown-grey stone, two round towers linked by an archway. The portcullis was raised enough to allow horse riders to pass under and a man with the arms of a black eagle on his shield was keeping a lazy watch on the traffic. He barely glanced at the two pilgrims.

'Two?' asked the hostel-keeper. He had a strange accent, not French.

'Two,' said Roger.

The dark-bearded man took a key and led them out of the crammed hall, which formed one side of a courtyard. There was a small well in the centre. The stables were the second side and a galleried building made the other side. The host let the way up the steps onto the gallery and opened the first door.

'Any others?'

'No.'

'Thank you.'

The little room had just one bed, a chest, a chamber pot, a pewter jug of water and a wooden washing bowl. The shuttered window was aimed straight at the setting sun, bathing the room in yellow light.

'Seen worse,' said Peter.

'Seen worse,' agreed Roger, casting off his bag. 'Oh, dear Lord God in Heaven, that feels better.'

Peter laughed and pulled his own bag off. 'I feel as if I've been carrying that since Hertford.'

'Have you not?'

'No, only since Canterbury.'

'Such a difference.'

'We should get some food.'

'I could do that.'

The hall was busy and full of the smell of people and roasting meat, the noise of half a dozen languages and laugher, the smoke of the fire and the clatter of tableware.

'I thought that The Star was busy,' said Peter.

'Your tavern?'

'A little inn on the North Road, yes. Many of my neighbours work the fields, the inn is the only place we can meet.'

A servant placed two plates of roast boar, bread, cheese and two mugs of ale on their table and smiled broadly at Roger.

'I think she likes you,' said Peter.

Roger shrugged. 'I couldn't... not yet.'

'Your wife passed?'

'Plague.'

'I am sorry, Roger.'

'I survived. That's why I came here. Do you have a wife?'

'Katherine. But she did not want to make such a long journey.'

'It is long and dangerous. Not much place for a woman.'

A group of people nearby started singing.

'I can't understand that,' said Peter.

'Italian, I think.'

'Do you know any good songs?'

'Not with women in the room.'

Peter laughed. 'Save them for the road home.'

'I will.'

The next morning was cold and wet, the rain overnight had lashed against the shutters until just after dawn. The pilgrims were already groping their groggy way out of the hostel towards the towering octagonal basilica.

There was a brown-habited monk waiting outside and, when about fifty had gathered, gave a short speech in Latin that sounded like a welcome. He then gave a blessing and invited the pilgrims to enter the great church. At the door was another monk with a wooden box. The box had a slot in the top and the pilgrims each paid to step into the huge, almost silent space. The only noise was that of a priest intoning prayers. Another was walking around swinging a censor of incense. Almost every surface was covered in bright mosaics in gold, red and blue, totally unlike an English church with its painted stone. An ancient-looking stone throne stood looking across the empty space between the doors and the altar, covered in a faded and battle-torn flag.

There was another blessing and the pilgrims were shown around the side to beside the altar, where two more monks were waiting. Behind the altar was a great golden chest, large enough almost to be a coffin, built like a small church, with small spires on the top, open doors and golden figures of Jesus Christ, the Virgin Mary and other scenes covered its surface.

'Vigilia et repetere post me,' said one monk softly. He turned to the altar, made the sign of The Cross, bowed his head to the reliquary, bowed to the floor and crawled to the open doors. He knelt up to be able to see inside and recited the Lord's Prayer before standing and walking aside. The first monk pointed to one of the pilgrims, who copied the pattern and, as he walked away, another person was chosen to go forwards. Roger was the fifth chosen and shivered in anticipation as he went forwards. When he was finished, he looked across at Peter and made a signal that he was going to find some food. Peter smiled and gave him a short bow, which was returned.

Half of the group had gone before Peter was finally chosen. Suddenly, the excitement grew. He made the sign of The Cross, bowed to the floor and crawled to the doors. The open space was a little more than a foot square. Inside, there was a blue folded cloak, white swaddling bandages, a small brown-grey cloth and a larger one that seemed to be stained with blood. He could barely think the words of the prayer as he gazed upon the very things worn by Jesus Christ, the son of God, his mother the Blessed Virgin Mary and St John the Baptist, testifier to The Light. He almost stumbled as he stood. The monk beckoned him aside, he was taking too long. He tottered across, still awestruck.

'Can I stay to pray?'

The monk nodded and pointed to a chapel nearby. Peter went in, knelt in front of the small altar and prayed until past noon.

Medieval help section

Aix-la-Chapelle- Medieval French city, now the city of Aachen in Germany.

Cathedral at Aix-la-Chapelle- Aachen Cathedral has an amazing eight-sided dome and a towering choir section behind it. Maybe the most fantastic-looking church in Europe.

Crécy- A battle in 1346 between the English and French. The English lost after the French attacked before they were ready and were overwhelmed by the English archers.

Crusades- The Holy Wars organised and financed by several popes between the Tenth and Thirteen Centuries, often aimed at conquering Jerusalem, which was ruled by Muslims.

Holy Land- The Medieval name for Israel and Palestine, called this because it was the country that Jesus lived in. The city of Jerusalem was believed to be the centre of the whole world.

Latin- The language of the Medieval Church, even in England, was Latin. There were huge arguments, even riots, when people tried to translate the Bible into other languages and do church services in English.

Nottingham- City in England. It had (and still has) a major castle and a cathedral. In Medieval England, it was important for the making of lace and clothes.

Pilgrim- A pilgrim is a religious traveller, in Medieval times they often went to famous sites because of stories or relics that were kept in churches.

Plague- The Bubonic Plague, known as the Black Death, came in waves all through the Thirteenth Century right up to the Seventeenth Century. Some plagues, such as 1348, killed up to 40% of people in England.

Poitiers- A battle in 1348, won by the English. Afterwards, the English captured the French King and most of his knights.

Portcullis- A wood and metal grid used to block gateways to help defend a gatehouse or castle entrance. Sometimes there was a gate behind it and there was often more than one portcullis.

Reliquary- A container for holy relics. The one in Aachen is still there. Reliquaries were all over the medieval world and contained things as strange as milk from the Virgin Mary (England), Jesus's underwear (Aachen) and enough fingers for St Peter to have about twenty on each hand.

Vigilia et repetere post me- Latin for "watch and copy me". Most pilgrims would have been in a place for the first time so someone would have to show them what to do.

Ware- Town in Hertfordshire, England. On Ermine Street, now the A10, from London to Lincoln.

Wollaton- Village in Nottinghamshire, probably occupied since the Roman times, now part of Nottingham city.

Activities and work ideas

Things to do are in bold

Ancient Greece

The Gods

There might have been as many as 100 Greek Gods. Below is a prayer from a Spartan priest to Ares, the god of war.

Ares, exceeding in strength, chariot-rider, golden-helmed, doughty in heart, shield-bearer, Saviour of cities, harnessed in bronze, strong of arm, unwearying, mighty with the spear, O defence of Olympus, father of warlike Victory, ally of Themis, stern governor of the rebellious, leader of righteous men, sceptred King of manliness, who whirl your fiery sphere among the planets in their sevenfold courses through the aether wherein your blazing steeds ever bear you above the third firmament of heaven; hear me, helper of men, giver of dauntless youth! Shed down a kindly ray from above upon my life, and strength of war, that I may be able to drive away bitter cowardice from my head and crush down the deceitful impulses of my soul.

Find the words you don't know or understand, find out what they mean and rewrite the prayer more simply.

*   *   *

Olympic Games

The Olympic festival was originally a celebration for the chief of the Greek Gods, Zeus. The first games, held at Olympia in the south-west of Greece, probably in 776BC and continued for over 700 years uninterrupted. Games were held every four years and all wars were stopped to allow the competitors to travel without danger. The Olympic Truce was so important that no Greek city violated it. The Olympics were one of 4 Panhellenic Games (the other three were the Pythian Games at Delphi in honour of Apollo, the Nemean Games at Nemea and the Isthmian Games at Corinth in honour of Poseidon) but came to be the most important.

Politicians used the games to announce alliances and priests would offer sacrifices. Winners were given wreaths or crowns made of olive wreaths, symbolising peace and victory coming together. At first, only men could compete but boys (aged 10 to 15) were allowed to compete in later years. Athletes wore no clothes, an idea introduced by Sparta.

Women had their own games at Olympia: the Heraean Games but they only had footraces. There were 3 age groups and they wore special tunics, unfortunately very little information survives about these games.

The main events were:
- *Stade*- a race of about 200 metres
- *Diaulos*- 400 metre race
- *Dolichos*- a race of about 5 kilometres

- Wrestling
- Pentathlon- *stade,* wrestling, javelin throwing, discus throwing and long jump
- Boxing
- Chariot race with 2 horses
- Chariot race with 4 horses
- Horse racing
- *Pankration-* a combat sport like a cross between boxing and wrestling, a bit like modern MMA
- Hoplite race- a *diaulos* in full armour and weapons
- Separate discus, shotput, javelin and long jump competitions

You can try some of these yourself if you've got space!

- Long jump

There was no run-up in the Ancient Olympics. Hold a weight, about a kilogram, in each hand. Stand on a line, swing your arms a few times and jump forwards, landing with both feet together. The distance is measured from where your toes start to where they finish.

- Shotput

You'll need a decent-sized stone, a brick or a weight. Make sure you've got space to throw. Stand on the line/mark/in a hoop, hold the shot over your shoulder and throw. The distance is measured from the line to the furthest end of the shot.

- Wrestling

Be careful with this one! And you need someone to practice against. You need a circle about 2-3 metres across. The idea is to push the other person totally out of the circle. You can't touch the other person on the head or below the bellybutton.

In 393 AD, the Roman Emperor Theodosius I decided that the Olympic Games were a 'vile pagan exhibition' and ordered them stopped.

Imagine the Ancient Olympics were like a modern one. Design a poster to advertise the games to get people to come and watch.

You could describe the events, the religious festival or whatever you'd like to do highlight. Make sure you make it clear that only men and boys can go!

Ancient Rome

Roman soldiers

Roman soldiers didn't go home very often. Legionaries served for 25 years and might have only got leave (holiday) once or twice every 2 or 3 years. The best way to keep in touch with your parents or family was to write.

Imagine you're a Roman soldier posted to Britain having been serving in the desert. Write a letter to someone about your move. Think about the differences between the desert and Britain, what your new friends in the Legion might be like and what your journey was like.

*　　　*　　　*

Mosaics

Mosaics were a fantastic Roman art form, making pictures and patterns out of small pieces of pottery tile. Being a mosaic artist or *Artifex* required a lot of training and a lot of practice, just like art today.

An *artifex* who was particularly good would travel around doing the mosaics in big houses, villas and temples. If you were good enough, you might even be called to Rome to work for a senator or even the Emperor!

You can make your own mosaic.
You need:
- Coloured paper, card, foil etc

- Glue
- A pencil
- A frame, paper plates are ideal

Cut the paper, card, foil into small pieces. Use as many colours as you like, try and make the pieces different shapes and use as many colours as you want.
Draw your design on the frame, use the internet to find some ideas.
Glue the pieces onto the frame to make your design.

Saxons and Vikings

Some Viking thinking

Q1- How do you think Vikings would have thought about Britain? Would it have been better or worse than Denmark or Norway? How would the time of year have made a difference?

Q2- Where would Vikings have landed? What would they have looked for? What would they have avoided? What would they need to take on a raid?

Q3- Write a modern business plan for a Viking trip to Britain, from a warrior to his chief. Tell him (or her, Viking chiefs could be women) what you will need, where you want to go, how you will get there and how long it will take. Tell them who you want to go with you and why they are needed. Most importantly, explain the risks and the potential rewards.

Ask your teacher to send your business plan to Peter Sawyer Living History and Tørvald Ragnarsson will write back!

Medieval

Medieval dinner time!

Unless you were rich, medieval food was very boring and repetitive. Very few people could afford meat, in fact cheese was often called 'white meat'. Most food was vegetables, herbs and other things that people could grow themselves.

This simple recipe called pottage has dozens of different types and changed according to what was available. It's not 100% accurate but gives you a good idea.

This is for 4 people, takes about 20 minutes, needs only 1 pan and uses simple measurements! This recipe is vegan but there's options to make it a little bit meaty if you want to.

Ingredients

- Ξ   2 teaspoons of oil for frying
- Ξ   1 onion
- Ξ   2 cloves of garlic
- Ξ   A big handful of mushrooms per person, chopped into bitesize bits
- Ξ   Half a white cabbage, chopped into little pieces
- Ξ   A tin of haricot, cannellini or flageolet beans in water
- Ξ   A tablespoon of grains (pearl barley, quinoa, whatever you have) per person
- Ξ   Vegetable stock, enough to cover everything
- Ξ   Fresh parsley, thyme and chives (Or a teaspoon of dried mixed herbs)
- Ξ   Salt and pepper, about a teaspoon of each

Optional

ɸ   A rasher of bacon per person, chopped into small pieces

ɸ   Replace half the oil with a teaspoon of butter

ɸ   Gravy granules to make it thicker

How to make it

Φ   Chop the onion and garlic up small and put them in a saucepan with the oil (and butter if you're using it), put it on middle heat (3 out of 5). Stir them a bit every minute or so.

Φ   ONLY IF YOU'RE USING BACON: When they've been sizzling for about 4 minutes, add the bacon and cook this for about 3 minutes until it's done.

Φ   Add the mushrooms and give them a stir for a minute or 2.

Φ   Add the vegetable stock, salt and pepper, beans, cabbage and grains. Let it cook for about 5 minutes, stirring it all together.

Φ   DRIED HERBS: Add them now!

Φ   There should be quite a bit of soupy broth. If there isn't, add a little bit of water. If you want it a bit thicker, add a bit of vegetable or chicken gravy granules.

Φ   FRESH HERBS: Add them right at the last moment and cook for about 1 minute.

Φ   Eat it with a spoon with bread for dipping. Make sure you've got enough bread to mop it all up!

Printed in Poland
by Amazon Fulfillment
Poland Sp. z o.o., Wrocław